Weird Weather

Frozen Wonders

Joanne Mattern

Enslow Publishing

Please visit our website, www.enslow.com. For a free color catalog of all our high-quality books,
call toll free 1-800-398-2504 or fax 1-877-980-4454

Published in 2027 by
Enslow Publishing
2544 Clinton Street
Buffalo, NY 14224

Cataloging-in-Publication Data
Names: Mattern, Joanne, 1963-.
Title: Frozen wonders / Joanne Mattern.
Description: Buffalo, NY : Enslow Publishing, 2027. | Series: Weird weather | Includes glossary.
Identifiers: ISBN 9781978549722 (pbk.) | ISBN 9781978549739 (library bound) | ISBN 9781978549746 (ebook)
Subjects: LCSH: Snow--Juvenile literature. | Blizzards--Juvenile literature. | Winter storms--Juvenile literature. | Freezes (Meteorology)--Juvenile literature. | Weather--Juvenile literature.
Classification: LCC QC926.37 M375 2027 | DDC 551.5784--dc23

Photos Credits: Cover, p.1 ©2020 Joe Belanger/Shutterstock.com; p.3 and throughout the book ©2020 Cherisha Kay Norman/Shutterstock.com; p.4 ©2016 Mazur Travel/Shutterstock.com; p.5 ©2021 BetterPhoto/Shutterstock.com; p.6 ©2008 Desintegrator/Shutterstock.com; p.6, p.7 ©2019 Martin Bartusek/Shutterstock.com; p.8 ©2017 Vladimir Rey/Shutterstock.com; p.9 ©2023 justkgoomm/Shutterstock.com; p.10 ©2018 DejaVuDesigns/Shutterstock.com; p.11, p.28 ©2018 PBouman/Shutterstock.com; p.12 ©2023 Applejak/Shutterstock.com; p.12, p.13 ©2024 Hawk777/Shutterstock.com; p.14© 2019 John McCormick/Shutterstock.com; p.15©2018 Razvan Vasile/Shutterstock.com; p.16 ©2025 Samuel Brandt/Shutterstock.com; p.17,p.28 ©2011 djgis/Shutterstock.com; p.18 ©2024 BarrieM/Shutterstock.com; p.19, p.29 ©2019 Ted Pendergast/Shutterstock.com; p.20, p.21 ©2017 C. Lee Parrish/Shutterstock.com; p.22 ©2024 Shy Radar/Shutterstock.com; p.22 ©2024 MantasVD/Shutterstock.com; p.23 ©2021 New Africa/Shutterstock.com; p.24, ©2023 Astrid Gast/Shutterstock.com; p.24, p.25, p.29 ©2023 Jasmine Sahin/Shutterstock.com; p.26 ©2023 Katvic; p.27, p.29 ©2025 Average Dad/Shutterstock.com

Printed in China

CPSIA compliance information: Batch #QSENS27: For further information, contact Enslow Publishing, New York, New York, at 1-800-398-2504.

TABLE OF CONTENTS

Words in the glossary appear in **bold** type the first time they are used in the text.

BURIED IN SNOW

The snow started falling in Iran on February 3, 1972. Snowstorms were not unusual in this country. But the 1972 blizzard would be one for the record books.

For seven days straight, the snow did not stop. More than 10 feet (three meters) of snow fell in the central and northern parts of the country. But that was nothing compared to the snow in the south. Parts of southern Iran recorded an astounding 26 feet (eight meters) of snow!

Soon, people were trapped inside their homes. There was no heat, no food, no power. They could not get out. The houses turned into places of death.

When the snow finally stopped, rescue crews were horrified at what they found. Houses, cars, and trucks were crushed under the heavy snow. In several villages, every person had died. Helicopters flew in to rescue the few people who had survived.

The Iran blizzard killed more than 4,000 people. It was a terrible show of frozen weather at its worst.

THE SNOW KEPT COMING

Rescuers had to stop their work when another blizzard struck two days later. They left bread out in the snow in case anyone had survived.

BLASTING BLIZZARDS

A blizzard is a special kind of snowstorm. These monsters are nothing like the few inches of snow that might fall in a normal storm. If a storm produces heavy snow for at least three hours, it might be a blizzard!

A blizzard also has high winds. To be a blizzard, a storm's winds must blow at speeds of at least 35 miles (56 kilometers) per hour. The snow and wind in a blizzard make **visibility** nearly impossible. You cannot see more than a quarter of a mile (400 meters) in front of you.

Blizzards form when low pressure from a storm system meets up with higher pressure outside the storm. This creates very strong winds. If the temperature is cold enough and the storm has enough **moisture**, heavy snow and high winds create a powerful storm.

Blizzards do a lot of damage. Snow buries sidewalks, roads, and train tracks. It is dangerous to drive or even walk. Heavy snow can also bring down trees and power lines.

People can be lost in a blizzard. They can't see where they are! They might freeze to death close to a shelter that they cannot see.

THE BIG FREEZE

Blizzards are dangerous to both people and animals. In 2013, a surprise blizzard struck South Dakota. More than 60,000 cattle and other livestock died where they stood in the fields.

PILING UP

Big snowstorms cause big snowdrifts. These drifts can bury cars and even buildings! Drifts happen when wind blows snow into huge piles. The Blizzard of 1888 buried parts of the eastern United States with 50-foot (15-meter) drifts.

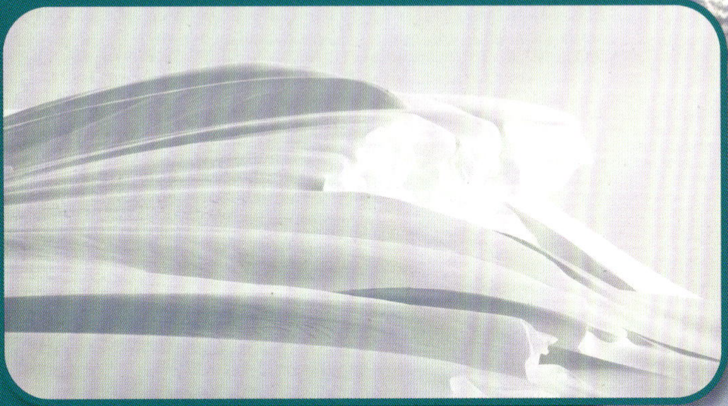

Mountains often get heavy snow that doesn't melt until spring. The snow lasts all winter, creating a snowpack. In 1927, Mount Ibuki in Japan was buried in a crazy amount of snow. The snowpack was more than 465 inches (11.8 meters) deep. That could be enough snow to bury a four-story building!

LIVING BY THE LAKE

The same snowstorm can produce different snow totals in different places. Areas near the Great Lakes in the United States are famous for how much snow they receive. This region is called the Snow Belt.

What is it about lakes and snow? It all has to do with temperature. When cold air moves across the warm waters of a lake, it causes moisture to rise. The air **condenses** and forms clouds. Colder air and warmer water can lead to snow ... lots of snow! Lake effect snow can fall as fast as five inches (12.7 centimeters) in an hour.

FUTURE STORMS

Some scientists think climate change will make lake effect snow even worse. That's because lakes will have warmer temperatures and less ice cover.

QUICK AND LOUD

Sometimes, an ordinary storm can turn **violent** in a hurry. Snowfall picks up, and so does the wind. It's like a mini blizzard! But a blizzard can last for hours or days. A snow squall usually lasts just 30 to 60 minutes.

Thunder and lightning usually happen in the summer. But you might hear thunder during a snowstorm too. Sometimes, warm air collides with cold, **unstable** air during a snowstorm. If conditions are just right, lightning will form inside a snow-filled cloud. And with lightning comes thunder! This strange **phenomenon** is called thundersnow.

OVER THE LAKE

Thundersnow is most common during lake effect storms because of the warm air rising from the water.

ICED UP

Snow is not the only frozen wonder to fall from the sky. Winter storms can also bring ice. And we're not talking about the ice cubes in your drink!

Ice storms start when warm air is trapped above a layer of cold air. When raindrops in warm air fall through the layer of freezing air near the ground, the rain freezes and turns to ice. And that ice can cause a big mess!

Ice storms do a lot of damage. The ice coats streets and sidewalks, making them **slippery**. It covers tree branches and power lines. When that happens, trees and lines can fall. The power might go out. Homes might be damaged.

WHAT'S THE DIFFERENCE?

Freezing rain and sleet might seem the same. The difference is in the timing. Freezing rain falls as liquid but turns into ice when it hits the cold ground. Sleet freezes in the air and falls as ice.

One of the worst ice storms in history struck the United States and Canada in 1998. Parts of upstate New York, northern New England, and eastern Canada were hit with more than three inches (seven centimeters) of ice. The storm lasted for days, freezing everything in its path.

The storm knocked down power lines and towers. Millions of people lost power. Some were without power for weeks. Roads were covered with ice. Buildings were damaged. Thousands of trees fell. At least 30 people died.

HELPING HANDS

*After the storm was over, people came from all over the United States and Canada to help **restore** power. Neighbors helped each other. Soldiers helped too.*

THUNDER ICE

People expect to see ice in the winter. Lakes and ponds might freeze. Icicles might hang from roofs. Or ice could coat the sidewalk, making your walk slippery. But one kind of ice is very different. This ice comes in pellets or chunks. And it usually falls in the summer! We are talking about hail.

Hail forms during a thunderstorm. Water droplets start to fall to Earth. But the strong winds inside the storm blow them up into colder air. The droplets freeze and fall. Then, they are blown upward again. Each time the droplets rise, they are covered with another layer of ice. Eventually, the ice is heavy enough to fall to the ground.

You might think big chunks of ice falling from the sky could be dangerous. You're right! Hail can dent cars. It can damage roofs and break windows. It can even kill people! In 1888, a hailstorm in India killed 246 people. The hail was described as being "as big as goose eggs and oranges."

Hailstones can be quite large. The biggest hailstone ever recorded in the United States fell in South Dakota in 2010. It was more than 18 inches (46 centimeters) around and weighed almost two pounds (0.9 kilogram).

HEAVY HAIL

Nebraska, Colorado, and Wyoming have the most hailstorms of any state in the U.S. They are often referred to as Hail Alley.

FROZEN AIR

Frozen wonders are created by frozen air. One of the largest masses of frozen air is the polar vortex. This area of low pressure and cold air sits above the North Pole. But it doesn't always stay there!

During the winter, freezing-cold air from the polar vortex often moves south to cover parts of the United States. The vortex brings very cold temperatures. Even warm places such as Florida have been hit with the polar vortex.

Winter is a time of frozen wonders, so bundle up! Whether it's cold weather, snow, or ice, any place can be hit by a big freeze!

WHAT AM I?

Can you guess what type of frozen wonder is shown in each photo? Look closely at these images and use the clues to help you figure it out. Then, check your answers below. How many did you get right?

1

I cause flashing lights and loud booms in the snow. What am I?

2

Brr! I'm full of cold winds and snow, and danger can strike when I come around. What am I?

3

My icy stones come down on a stormy summer day. Listen to me clatter and crash! What am I?

4

You might live somewhere warm, but watch out for a cold wave when my low pressure and frozen air come around! What am I?

5

I'm pretty and sparkly, but I'll make you slip and slide. What am I?

1. thundersnow; 2. blizzard; 3. hail; 4. polar vortex; 5. ice

GLOSSARY

condenses (kun-DEN-sez): changes from a gas to a liquid

moisture (MOYS-chur): dampness

phenomenon (fuh-NAH-muh-nahn): an unusual and remarkable event

restore (ri-STOR): to bring back

slippery (SLIP-ur-ee): hard to walk on

unstable (uhn-STAY-buhl): not steady; likely to change

violent (VY-uh-lent): strong and destructive

visibility (viz-uh-BIL-i-tee): the ability to see

FACT CHECK

1. A blizzard produces heavy snow for at least three ___________.
   a. hours b. days c. weeks
2. Sleet forms when ___________ falls through freezing air.
   a. snow b. water c. hail
3. Hail usually falls in the ___________.
   a. summer b. fall c. winter

Answers: 1. a, 2. b, 3. a

FURTHER READING

Bell, Samantha S. *Blizzards*. Abdo Reference, 2024.

Mattern, Joanne. *Blizzards*. BrightPoint Press, 2025.

Winch, Anne. *Ice Storms: Causes and Effects*. 12-Story Library, 2022.

ON THE INTERNET

Blizzards

https://kids.nationalgeographic.com/science/article/blizzards

This National Geographic Kids article explains what blizzards are and the destruction they can cause.

Winter Storms

www.weatherwizkids.com/weather-winter-storms.htm

This Weather Wiz Kids page describes the different kinds of winter storms, how they form, and how to stay safe.

INDEX

ABOUT THE AUTHOR

Joanne Mattern is the author of many books for children on a variety of subjects, including science, history, and biography. She loves writing about and experiencing weird weather events! Joanne loves to learn about people, places, and events and bring historical figures to life for today's readers. She lives in New York State with her family.